Shattering The Glasshouse: A Memoir

TAMIEKA SMITH

SHATTERING THE GLASSHOUSE

ISBN: 0692353984
ISBN-13: 978-0692353981

DEDICATION

This book is dedicated to all the purple warriors.
We have similar stories but come from different backgrounds.
One voice can change a life.
Every story is unique.
Few survive.
Some lose.
Here is my dedication to you.

SHATTERING THE GLASSHOUSE

CONTENTS

SHATTERING THE GLASSHOUSE

ACKNOWLEDGMENTS

If you are reading this, that means this book meant something to you to take the time to pick up and I am eternally grateful for that. I could not have done this without staying true to my faith. No matter how many times I have been tested, moments I just wanted to breakdown, technical glitches, or just not knowing how to say what I wanted to print, THANK GOD my baby is released to the world. Thank you for unconditional love and support to my dear family. Thank you for listening to those random rants and messages of reassurance to my friends. I hope that everyone take something away from this memoir to give them a different perspective about domestic violence. To my darling sons: You are my peace in the storms. I am so blessed to be your mother. I hope I have made you proud.

SHATTERING THE GLASSHOUSE

1 PRELUDE TO A KISS...OF DEATH

The fear he put in her made her afraid..."I will kill you if you ever lead astray."

He would do horrible things to her like punches to the face.

It all started mentally.

Situations made her question her ability.

Unable to think sensibly.

She thought it was meant to be.

All he wanted was control.

Fed her promises to have and to hold.

Get in her brain to fit his perfect mold.

"Get away from him." Is what they told.

She was too blind.

The abuse was over time.

The things he did to her was a crime.

One day she will see the sunshine.

Days of torture diffused by his smiles.

Then there comes a child.

The abuse stopped...for a while.

Those painful memories stored like a computer file.

Not capable of walk in my shoes, even for a mile.

She will drive to the road of freedom.

It was time to go back to where to came from.

The precious cargo included yes, an additional son.

But it's okay we hopped in the car; this time I'm done.

It's unfair for you to see these tears.

Time to let go of the fears.

Regained my strength to leave, this moment took years.

Nights before I thought I would be killed.
REPEATEDLY slammed my head against the bathroom mirror.
When his hands was around my neck, death appeared clearer.
I quietly recited, "Yea though I walk through the valley of the shadow of death…."
The Psalm amazingly kept me calm.
All of his jealousy, anger, and rage took center stage.
It was time to leave this dramatic play.
It took alot of courage for the day she went away.

2 THE WAKEUP CALL

I was so tired of this. Continually getting beat. Constantly being talked about. Walking on eggshells as if any wrong word, look, or practically anything would set him off. I laid in the bed that Friday night holding my neck in disbelief. I even went to the kitchen and looked at a knife. I shook my head no and went back to the bedroom we shared. I was NOT going out like that. HIs insecurities would be the death of me if I didn't do a dramatic change. But there was one (or two) little things that held me back. My kids are little people. Little people that witnessed their father doing the most horrific things to their mother.

This wasn't the American Dream. It was a nightmare. Holding onto something that didn't serve me. Holding onto someone that didn't even love himself. Now here I am, on the brink of death. This was when enough was enough. I cried myself to sleep for years. I even asked God to take me out my misery because I was too afraid to leave. The scent of him made me nauseous because I couldn't look at him without being disgusted.

Love or my idea of love was coming to an end.

A few hours ago, my head was getting banged into a bathroom mirror we shared. I could barely get my children in the house after work before being attacked. No, "Hey how was your day?" Or anything. He was obessed. Obessed in knowing ALL of the ins and outs to make sure I didn't do or say anything inappropriately as if I was his child.

We had already gone over everything with the phone call conversation. On the way home. Barely cared about how the kids was doing or me for that matter. Just wanted to know who, what, why, where, and when of my day. Just to make sure I didn't have a "work boyfriend." That was his theme mostly for beating me.

I told him, "I've never cheated on you so why do you continue on like this? Why do you have to always do this? Don't you see I want our family to succeed?"

He was blind. Insecure. Overbearing. Scary. But he was charming, caring, all of the things I thought I needed in a man.

The last words he said to me calmly, "Okay since you want to play games, you're going to get it when you get here." CLICK

I hung up the phone. I prayed to God please help me.

3 LOOKING DEATH IN THE EYE

I stepped in the house. I remember looking at the sand on the ground before going in wishing I was at a beach. Here I was only a couple hours away from my hometown in the Sandhills of North Carolina getting abused on the regular. Being at the point of let him just hurry up hit me, and hope that he doesn't hurt me too bad, I was mentally preparing myself. But nothing could prepare me for what happened that day.

"Get in the house." He calmly commanded. Pointed to the living room couch for me to sit.

I looked at him. I could see sweat trickling down his face. This wasn't his "usual" mad.

So again, he asked me what happened at work. I told him the same thing. No I don't have a work boyfriend. No I'm not interested in the guy that is training me at this new job. No we haven't went out to lunch ever. No he's not flirting with me. No I'm not leaving you. It felt like I was just going through the motions. Going through life but not living.

He yanked me up. His response was, "NO you not telling the whole story but you're going to talk today!" I put the kids in their room so they wouldn't see anything. He then proceeded with pulling me to our bedroom. He told me to look in the mirror in our bathroom. I looked. He then grabbed the back of my head and repeatedly slammed my head on the mirror with so much intensity, I was surprised it didn't break. "You care about how you look more than your own boys!" I yelled with tears flowing down my face, "No that's not true!!"

I felt so numb. I begged and pleaded for him to just stop. I wanted him to completely stop it. This started in February 2006 and now it's April 2010.

I was thrown on the bed. I looked at him in terror. He grabbed a pillow and smothered my face with it. It began.

The pillow didn't give him satisfaction. He used his hands. His hands was around my neck. I just wanted to breathe. I just wanted the pain to go away. I almost felt like surrendering. Then I thought about my boys, I want to see them be young men. Not one to abuse another but to love. If I didn't survive, my mother would have to bury me. My family would be saddened. The friends I had would be hurt. Others would have been shocked. I didn't care about him anymore. I cared more about me.

I prayed silently in my mind. The pressure of his hands was strong, but somehow I was able to calm in this insane situation.
Yea though I walk through the valley of the shadow of death, I shall fear no evil. Thy rod and thy staff shall comfort me.

I looked at him with tears. Then looked at the boys at the door. My hear just broke. I begged him to stop. When he finally moved his hands from around my neck, I just looked at him and asked, "Do you want your boys to do what you're doing to me?"

At that point it seems like he woke up from blacking out and realized what he did. He replied like he usually do with a the driest "I'm sorry, it won't happen again."

He was right. It wouldn't. I had to leave. We had to leave.

4 POINT OF NO RETURN

I came to the realization that it was time to plan an escape route. It felt like one of those fire escapes in New York. But I was trying to maneuver out of a living hell trying not to be notice or heard before it was too late. The caveat was that I had two babies. One in diapers and the other in pull ups. I knew I had to leave. But the question was how? I already had my mind made up that I don't care what kind of gestures he tries with me, there was no coming back.

The major thing about being abused is the control factor. It's a stronghold. A soul tie. An addiction just as strong as herion. Not just for the abuser but for the victim too. We get "used to it". Once the abuse feels out of control, they are weak. Like the cowardly lion.

I started thinking of my own escape route. It was like a play by play on Sporstcenter. I had to think quickly. After he finished choking me that night I didn't sleep. I had me ah ha moment. I was still in the scrubs from coming home from work. That would be my getaway. I knew he had to be at work before me. His mother and stepfather stayed across the street. I just prayed she didn't walk across the street and catch me packing up my little Mazda Protege. Because she knew. They all knew. But I was told, "He loves you and you have to just pray about it." It even questioned my faith at one time because I thought what God would allow "people of God" to just turn a blind eye? It wasn't the people around me that saved me. It by God's grace.
The plan was complete.

I was technically the breadwinner. I counted up the funds and knew that it would be a race to the bank. He wanted to be "as one" but really he wanted to be overbearing and know every financial move I was making.Again, he was obessed with me cheating. But I found hotel receipts from the bank account that we shared. Long phone call conversations on the cell phone account that we shared. Like my grandmother always says, when then accuser is accusing, check what they are hiding. I had the proof but still couldn't leave. But this brush with death was my wake up call.

Take all the money out of the account. Quit my job without warning. Don't tell my family or friends anything. Go far away if I have to for a little while. Whatever you do, just don't go back.

5 LEAVING

I knew I had to leave. There was no other option. He wasn't trying to change. I was done trying to change him. I'm not his mother. He's grown. In my mind, staying trying to make this family "work" just wasn't working. I thought it was honorable as if I was in a war getting my purple heart. Ironically, my purple heart was the purple that bleeds for domestic violence awareness. Ironically, I was in a battle with a stronghold of a demonic force. The beating that I took would be the last one. I had my mind made up.

Remember the escape route that I previously mentioned?

You have to get one to GET OUT. And stay out.

I like to use an acronym to help. Be S.A.F.E.

S-afe and Secure. When planning to leave an abusive relationship, know that this can be the most dangerous part of the relationship. Your safehouse will need to be one that is a place where you (including children) will need to feel safe. It need to be secure in case the abuser will try to find you. If at all possible, don't go to the usual places where the abuser can find you. Drastic times can be a cause for a drastic measure. It could even mean staying in a shelter. Go to a local library to do the searches for finding domestic abuse safehouses. Believe me, your abuser will look at your browsing history, cell phone history, banking history, even mileage on the car history. Get your hands on a prepaid phone to put in a getaway stash accessible to you when it's your time to leave.

A-ccountability Partner. Have someone you can trust to help you out of this situation. Just like your birthday, have a date in mind of leaving. They are in a way a midwife of helping you birth yourself into a new life. Sometimes it's not until you actually get that wakeup call like I did in Chapter 1. Your accountablity partner will help you stay on target for making sure that you leave. The domestic violence crisis lines can be your point of reference when helping you get out. The accountablity partner will also be the people that are your voice of reason to prevent you from going back when you start to miss this abuser. It is normal to feel this way. I didn't have an accountablity partner. I was my own. It's okay too. Plan it out and map it out. And just go.

F-earless Finance Stash. Have some money in a place that your abuser will not trace it. If you are able to open up a separate banking account, I strongly suggest you to do this. Instead of having cash stored around, get money orders and write them to yourself and get your own PO Box in a place that is open 24 hours so this way you have access at any time. Mail those money orders in your designated P.O. Box. Your receipts from the money orders should be also mailed to the PO Box. Don't use credit cards/debit cards. They are traceable. Lastly, have cash in a place where the abuser cannot get to it. It's risky doing because once it's lost, it is untraceable. Your fearless cash stash is your financial resource to help you get back on your feet.

E-ssential Documents. The essential documents that most people forget about when leaving unexpectedly. Make sure you have your (including children) forms of identification. This includes picture IDs, birth certificates,and anything of significance. You may have to leave without a trace.

This is the time that you will have a boldness like never before.

6 UGLY FACES OF DOMESTIC VIOLENCE

As you can imagine, nothing is pretty about Domestic Violence. There are many underlying layers just like an onion when it comes to this. It's not so black and white. I want to inform of the gray areas too in order to be aware of those red flags that can potentially save a loved one's life or even your own.

For one, when it's too good to be true, it usually in. An abuser never comes in the form of horns on their head to give you the ultimate red flag. It will come in every way you can ever imagine. The "guy or girl" of your dreams. Incredibly charming. Will be romantic. Say all the right things. Do all the right things. Have you thinking, "Where have you been all of my life?" Even thanking God for someone like this. That is until the true colors come out. Please know this: an abuser is manipulative. They will use their charming personality to rush you into a relationship like tomorrow cannot wait for itself. They will close you into making quick, life altering decisions without a steady pace. Discussions of the future from 0 to 100. Next thing you know, you could be living together, having an account and "In too deep" before even realizing it. I like to call it Fools Rushing In.

A relationship of substance takes time. Never rush into sex, love, finances, marriage, blending families, and the like without getting to know the person first. Learn how they are with their family. Many abusers are mentally unstable. Look for narcissistic behavior patterns. They look for victims that has low self-esteem, co dependent, or soul is broken. All of their moves comes with ulterior motives. These personality types never like to think they are wrong about anything. This can be very dangerous. I know that it was frustrating arguing with him because he carried this "I'm perfect" persona and I was the one who had all the issues to work on which clearly wasn't the case. It will feel like they are literally sucking the life out of you.

Once they have you, they want to control you. Their motive is to put you into isolation so that your world can revolve around them at all times. They may place the "blame game" on you saying that you don't spend enough time with them, your time is displaced with family, friends, or career when you are suppose to cater to their every need. It can almost feel like an adult child that you are dealing with. When you are not around them, they want to know who is around you. For instance, at work he wanted to know who I ate with and even asked me where everyone sat at. I know, ridiculous but it's true. I thought I was being the good girlfriend being honest without hesitation. The thing is with a narcissist, something will always be wrong. They will even control your church going, what you wear (including makeup), and also to the extent of checking internet history, cell phone usage, and mileage usage.

An abuser is incredibly jealous. Let me say this. In no way is jealousy "cute". It is a clear sign of insecurity on their behalf. Your entire relationship will mean you trying to perform surgery to "fix" this. You are coming in as a superhero to fix a narcissist. They have to want to fix themselves before you spend anytime trying to prove your love and loyalty. A jealous person is not interest in nothing you are doing that doesn't include you spending your undivided attention on them. According them, you can be the biggest flirt with anyone around. Accusations can be linked to family members. Those random pop up at the jobs can become creepy. (I'll tell you more about that later).

Lastly, victim blaming (similar to rape culture) is prominent in the domestic violence culture. I remember discussing some gruesome details with people. Then asked, "Well what did YOU do?!" It used to anger me. How passive aggressive it is to displace the blame to me. I had to look at it from a different scope. It is still hard for some to imagine that someone could act in such a way without being under the influence of drugs or alcohol. Just a person with a cunning, charming yet evil spirit could even exist is too much for some to imagine. The truth is, a person who is abusive theme is control. It is their fear of losing the person in the relationship which roots back to childhood. You will feel like you are constantly walking on eggshells. The dysfunction will even feel functional. Get to know who you are loving before loving them.

Here are some forms of abuse:

Physical-causing bodily harm without remorse, or with an empty apology. The pain can include pain, discomfort, or injury.

Sexual-common after physical attacks. Forced sexual encounters and/or humiliating the victim that may be degrading.

Emotional-constant name calling. Have the victim feel worthless or stupid by their actions. Use silent treatment as punishment to the other person.

Psychological-may threaten suicide if the person decides to leave the relationship. Treated like a child or servant. Instills fear in the victim.

Spiritual-may act like they agree with your religious preference then later tries to keep you from religious activities.

Verbal-withholds important information, name calling, threatens the person and/or family members, constantly expressing distrust.

Financial-misuse of money, controlling of financial decisions, or withholding funds to justify their reckless spending.

7 ATTACKED

When a person is attacked by the one they "love", it is one that they could never forget. It is life altering. Damage is done beyond the surface which can take years to recover from. The same person you love betrayed your trust and violated you. Once they stop, they may apologize only to do it again. Some abusive relationships stop after the first attack. However, many keep going. I understand how one can sleep with the promise of hope of you one love changing so you can be that ideal relationship with kids and home picket fence. Not everything is picture perfect. In order to have a happy, healthy relationship, learn how some of my encounters made me be more aware of what is love and what is not.

Valentine's Day 2006.
It was my first job after relocating and moving in with him. There wasn't a lot of stores in this small country town, so I went to a Dollar Store to show my appreciation of his love. I got off a little early and decided to pick up a Valentine's Day gift. It was our first Valentine's Day together. Unbeknownst to me, it would be the first of something else. Immediately when I opened the door, he asked angrily, "Where was I at?" No pleasantries. Just anger all over his face. With the gifts still in my hand, I told him I went to the store. It was like a knee jerk reaction. He slapped me. Hard. The sound still replays. I remember crying uncontrollably. I said this is what I doing and pulled out the gifts. Happy Valentine's Day. It was such a beautiful sunny day. It felt like my world was crushing in on me. How could someone that love me do this to me? He said nonchalantly, "You can go back to your mothers if

you want. I won't do it again." I believed him with a tiny glimmer of hope. It was only the beginning of a broken record.

Inventory.
While the pressures of this relationship was getting stressful, my outlet was when I was away from him at work. The first job I picked up was on assignment doing inventory for different local grocery stores. It required some out of state travel on company vans. It was a team of us. But of course, he didn't like the idea of me being out of his "sight". And I would hear of it. He would always of accuse me of having a work relationship with one of guys I worked with. The fear was immediately set in after the Valentine's Day episode and wasn't a sociable person while working. Although I was the naturally laid back type, I just decided it was best for me to be like that. To prevent any trouble. One day we were on assignment close by my home. I was focused on scanning cans and looked up. There he was looking at me with intensity. Just so happen, there was a guy working on the same aisle on the other side. He stuck around until it was time for lunch. We walked over to the other side of the shopping center for lunch.The first topic of conversation was this other guy on the aisle. The accusations started. I told him nothing was going on. I got attacked later that day. Soon after I quit that job.

Warehouse.
Another job I was able to get quickly from quitting the inventory job. This was light manufacturing work on second shift. I liked the steady pace of the job. I started to develop friendships with a couple females. It didn't take long before the accusations began again. One night he popped up at my job alongside a coworker of his. I didn't know this until later. I went back on the line early and heard people say that it was dangerous for someone to try to come into the back where we worked. For some reason, it my gut I had a feeling it was him. And it was.

Another night I was picked up from work. It was very dark that night. Something didn't feel right. He usually picked me up but for some reason he decided to go a different route. A route that was reclusive and scary. We started talking. He never looked directly at me. Then he started arguing. It was always about the same subject. He thought I was cheating on him. Never the case but always the theme. The car slowed down by some trees. He yelled then punched me in the face, "If you want to act like a hoe, I will treat you like one!" In disbelief, I responded, "What are you talking about? I didn't do anything but work." He demanded me to strip off my clothes. I was pushed out the car. I felt so numb. I stood there trembling, crying, praying for this to stop. I pleaded with him to please stop. I told him, "I love you, why are you acting like this?" That angered him more. I slowly took my shirt off. There I stood, in the wee hours of night somewhere in the country woods gazing at the starts asking to myself if God still existed. He demanded that I get back in the car calmly. I couldn't believe that he was sexually aroused by his horrendous actions. By the time we got back home, I laid in the bed feeling numb allowed him to do whatever he want to do just so I could forget about this nightmare.

I thought the abuse would stop over time. I thought having his kids would soften his heart. I lived in a state of perfectionism but it didn't matter to him what I did. It was nearly five years of episodes such as this. I had to shatter the glasshouse to let others know this is so common. Relationships like this are not healthy. One day crazy the other day normal. It was like dealing with a split personality type. I'm thankful to God for his saving grace throughout all of those years.

See, I am doing a new thing! Do you not perceive it? I am making a way in the wilderness and streams in the wasteland.
Isaiah 43:19 (NIV).

8 FIGHTING BACK

God said that he would do a new thing but the months after leaving no one could prepare me for. It was like being in the trenches fighting my way out.

A quick recap from the chapter Looking Death in the Eye: For some reason, I knew that leaving would be dangerous. It wasn't until afterwards I realized that when a victim leaves an abuser is the most dangerous times of their lives. The night when he first violently slammed my head against the bathroom mirror, then to forcibly have his hands around my neck really did it for me. That was my moment of realization that I cannot change him and I have to save us. My kids didn't deserve to grow up in this kind of environment. When he told me, "I'm sorry, it won't happen again." He was right. It wouldn't. And it didn't.

I left and packed everything I could possibly think of. I pretended to oversleep because I knew he had to be at work before I did. I knew God was giving me some saving grace. I went back to my mothers momentarily. It was hard not to be predictable but I felt a little less anxious. I decided to take as much money that I could and go to Texas with family for a little bit. It was a couple weeks. I didn't really have a plan but I had my life. The fog from my mind was removed. I felt free again. But, I was angry. As hell. I needed an attitude adjustment. I had it in my mind no one would push me over again. It took some time to get a handle on that. God always have a way to teach you valuable lessons.

Nevertheless, I didn't need to run away. I needed to face my abuser and move on with my life. So the boys and I went back to NC. I needed to let him know it wasn't okay to do what he did.

The first order of business was getting an order of protection. It was the first time I actually felt emancipated from the strongholds of this abusive person. They granted me a temporary one which meant I had to face him again.

My grandfather told me something that was like an "aha" moment. He told me to write down everything that he did to me. So I did. I found my voice.I remembered being so angry and frustrated about him acting like nothing happened. That was my way to have physical evidence.

Back in NC, I went to the county that we stayed in. Tried to file a report of the things that he done to me. Remember the attack of the wilderness? It was so brutal that the magistrate told me there was a possibility of him filing criminal charges. All I had to do was go to the sheriff's office. I did. Only to hit a brick wall. "Why you never reported this?" "Why you wait so long to file this?" "Why now, you sound like a bitter woman trying to retaliate on your ex."

The conversation had me livid. I wanted to slap the man in uniform. Thankfully, my grandfather was in the office with me. We knew it wasn't going anywhere. Have a nice day.

So about a month later, I had to go back to face him. I had time to prepare. Even tried to get a lawyer. I ended up defending myself that day. I put on my best two piece professional suit I owned. I knew that my story would not go unnoticed. When I saw that he had his own lawyer, that angered me more. I had to depend on government assistance checks to even be able to get some diapers. I had to quickly get back on my feet regardless of the situation. It was hard to grieve but all the emotions was there when it was my time. My 4'11 self was a powerhouse that day. I used the smarts that God gave me to make his lawyer and his client look silly. He had a history of abuse. I found out in the later part of our relationship. I asked him about it. And almost lied under oath. I had to remind him of where he was. I looked over at his lawyer. Red as a beet. I walked back to my table. All you could hear was the click of my heels.

Then he lawyer called me to the stand. He asked me what happened. I had to relive what happened to me in a tearful testimony. I looked at my abuser square in the eye and told him, "I'm not afraid of you ANYMORE! I have a gun permit and won't be scared to use it!" Of course the judge had to tell me to settle down. I just wanted to let him know that it wasn't okay. So many strangers that was in there said I did a wonderful job and asked me was I in law school. Even the clerk was impressed. When you all you have is strength after losing so many years of your life to abuse, it will even surprise yourself.

9 HOMELESS...REALLY?!

Humble yourselves before the Lord, and he will lift you up.
James 4:10 (NIV)

One of the biggest lessons I learned was a lesson in humility. Looking back, I wasn't pleasant to be around the first few months of leaving the dysfunction. I didn't want to be around me in that time. Still, I couldn't have peace. Without peace, it was difficult to look for a stable job, or even to have an action plan. I was depressed. Dealing with symptoms of post traumatic stress.

I found myself at a shelter. It did not make sense to other people, but it made perfect sense to me. I knew without a shadow of doubt that this would make a way for us. I did not care what family and friends said. I was already dealing with guilt, shame, and a lack of self-worth. I didn't have anything else to lose.

Those 10 months of staying in a shelter proved how strong I was. I opened up and got therapy. The things I was going through made sense to the therapist. I wasn't going crazy. It was just a process. I didn't need to medicate myself with dealing with wrong type of guys, drinking binges, or ignoring the reality I face. I got to the realness of life. Once again, I fought back. Took charge of my life. Even walked to church when my family had my boys on Sunday's. This relationship with God nobody could touch. The determination I had no one could remove. I knew I would be a "comeback kid".

It's funny how the things we take for granted means a lot more when we appreciate it in a period of rock bottom. I remember getting my first set of wheels after leaving the relationship. I proudly parked my car in the parking lot of the shelter. My first interview and landing the job felt like something out of a movie. I smiled getting off the bus. No one even knew I was in the situation I was in. We didn't "look" that way. My life forever changed once I was able to sign a lease all by myself. I was finally free. We regained our life back.

10 IT'S OKAY TO TALK TO SOMEBODY

To keep thoughts and feelings bottled in is not healthy. When a person is dealing with so many circumstances, it is best to have healthy outlets. A victim of domestic violence is very vulnerable to go into another toxic relationship if they don't allow themselves to heal. As crazy as it sounds, the dysfunction is functional.

It is important to have someone with a unbiased opinion. When dealing with matters of the heart, it is like performing open heart surgery to repair yourself to a better quality of life. You have to fix what is broken so it won't happen again. There can be so much scrutiny to speak with a therapist even in this day and age, but it makes a world of difference to speak with someone about what is going on in the inside.

My suggestion would be to speak with someone that has the experience of helping domestic violence victims. They know what to look out for and can provide you with effective ways to heal. Going to support groups makes you feel like you are not alone in the process. Just as it is important to be around other people, don't isolate yourself from the world. If you do that, it is unconsciously going back to the same symptoms of the dysfunction without even going back to the abuser.

I even wrote out my feelings when I felt like I couldn't speak to anyone. Post traumatic stress is not just for the military. It can have you feeling so out of place and nervous doing normal functions. It took awhile for me to stop looking in the rearview mirror or looking over my shoulder thinking that he is somewhere around looking for me. The fear subsided. The insomnia eventually went away. The feelings of shame eventually left. Find healthy ways to cope. Take as much time YOU need to heal. As frustrating as it could be for someone to tell you, "Just get over it", have compassion for their level of understanding. There is no time schedule for getting over abuse. Understand you will be misunderstood. That's okay.

11 FORGIVENESS

Forgiveness can be a delicate topic. It's very necessary to forgive. Defined, it is mentioned that it is the willingness to forgive. I will say it many times in this chapter because it is a very important one.

It doesn't have to be about abuse. Anyone that has done you wrong or you've done the wrong to another will have to let go the burden of bitterness. It's time FOR you to GIVE. It's time to you to give yourself a second chance at life. It's for them, it's for you! One of the things I had to understand was apologies are not those where you are waiting for someone to tell you they are sorry. They already know that. It's when a person has the humility to actually let go and let God do the work. Not to live in a state where you are wishing on their downfall, but when you pray for their deliverance for causing harm to another or potentially themselves. Forgiveness is not a weak emotion. It is one of the most powerful acts to give another. They are no longer in control of how you move forward in your life. It is when you have allowed yourself to be happy again. It is when you no longer sit in the VIP section of the guilt trip. That is no longer a destination for you. Live for today. Especially when children are involved.

Weeping may endure for only a night, but joy comes in the morning. Psalm 30:5.

12 ACCOUNTABILITY

Live for today but don't make the same mistake twice. When I was in the abusive relationship, I went back. It's normal. When fear is instilled, you will actually be afraid to function without the other person. Immediately it becomes codependent. Please be advised. When an abuser wants to come back into their web of deception and manipulation, they will do and say anything to "win" you over.

The period of being single is a time to love yourself again. Date yourself. Having self-worth doesn't include someone else seeing your worth. That is something you will have to know from within. Be accountable for you.

Being accountable includes knowing what to look out for when it's time to date again. The red flags are always there if we allow ourselves to pay attention to them.

Going through a situation means that you are still passing through the situation. I gained so much from surviving an abusive relationship:

Forgiveness

Never take life for granted

Own your story

Live for today

It's okay to succeed

A mustard seed of faith changes things

Healing takes time.

ABOUT THE AUTHOR

From Durham, North Carolina this petite woman used her voice in a strong way by being an advocate and survivor of domestic violence. Her story landed in Huffington Post Woman from her feature in Unconventional Apology. She turned her childhood past time to make writing a living with published works.

She continues her advocacy as an ambassador of 10Blessings and a

CoFounder of Sisters Pushing Sisters International. In her spare time she enjoys traveling with her children and trying out new food.

Affectionately called "Ms.Wordsmith" she created Wordsmith Books to sought out her self publishing endeavors to bring words to your world.

Stay connected!
TamiekaSmith.com
Instagram @TamiekaSmith
Twitter/Periscope @MsWordSmith

For booking information info@tamiekasmith.com

P.O. BOX 1858
APEX, NC 27502

www.ingramcontent.com/pod-product-compliance
Lightning Source LLC
Chambersburg PA
CBHW061759040426
42447CB00011B/2380